WE ARE NOT AMUSED

We Are Not Amused

Victorian views on pronunciation
as told in the pages of *Punch*

DAVID CRYSTAL

Bodleian Library
UNIVERSITY OF OXFORD

First published in 2017 by the Bodleian Library
Broad Street, Oxford OX1 3BG

www.bodleianshop.co.uk

ISBN   978 1 85124 478 2

Text © David Crystal, 2017

All images, unless specified on p. 85,
© Bodleian Library, University of Oxford, 2017.

David Crystal has asserted his right to be identified as the author of this Work.

Cover design by Dot Little at the Bodleian Library
Designed and typeset in 11 on 14 Bulmer
by illuminati, Grosmont
Printed and bound in China by C&C Offset Printing Co. Limited
on 115 gsm YuLong paper

British Library Catalogue in Publishing Data
A CIP record of this publication is available from the British Library

CONTENTS

INTRODUCTION

According to Princess Alice, in a 1977 interview, her grandmother Queen Victoria never uttered the famous words attributed to her. Alice actually once asked her, and was told 'I never said it'. Of course, this could have been faulty memory or evasive discomfort, but whether the Queen said it or not the comment has come to epitomize the supposed stiffness and severity of the Victorian age. It was an age that the writers and cartoonists of *Punch* relentlessly pilloried, and nowhere more so than in relation to the way people spoke.

In the sixty years between its first issue in 1841 and the death of the Queen in 1901, jokes about the changes, quirks and fashions affecting English usage provide one of *Punch*'s most fruitful veins of acerbic humour. The idiosyncrasies of pronunciation were a particular source of amusement to Victorians, especially the way in which social classes could be identified by their vowels and consonants. Cockney speakers were the primary target, but there was plenty of ammunition left over for the Scots, foreigners, Americans, aristocrats and virtually any notable group whose speech didn't conform to the cultured norm that had evolved during the early 1800s – what would later be known as 'Received Pronunciation' (RP).

Punch, of course, was not the only publication to show regional and social speech in action. In the nineteenth century, rural accents were a particular source of fascination to novelists and poets. George Eliot, Emily Brontë, Charles Dickens and many others captured the local speech of their characters – Luke in *The Mill on the Floss*, Joseph in *Wuthering Heights* and (probably the most famous of all) the Wellers, father and son, in *The Pickwick Papers*, whose *w* and *v* substitutions have even earned them a presence in books of quotations: 'a coachman may be on the wery amicablest terms with eighty mile o' females, and yet nobody think that he ever means to marry any vun among them' (Mr Weller, in

vii

chapter 52). But relatively little of England's rural diversity is found in *Punch*, whose writers – presumably with an editorial eye on readership and sales – focused on the accents most often encountered in the capital.

This book illustrates the features of pronunciation that preoccupied the contributors to the magazine for over half a century. We see nineteenth-century English linguistic nature reflected in its pages. I like to think, 150 years on, that we have developed a more tolerant and egalitarian climate in which accent diversity is seen in a positive light. But old attitudes die hard, and if the magazine were still around today I suspect its writers and cartoonists would continue to find an appreciative audience for their satire.

WHY THEN?

The way we speak had never received so much attention, satirical or serious, as it did in the nineteenth century. It was an age that began in Europe with the emergence of the academic study of language, in the form of philology, and ended – in Britain – with two major projects, James Murray's *Oxford English Dictionary* (begun in 1884) and Joseph Wright's *The English Dialect Dictionary* (published between 1896 and 1902). In addition to the lively interest in regional speech taken by the novelists and poets, there was a growing popular movement. By the end of the century, local dialect societies were beginning to be formed, the earliest in Yorkshire in 1897. In 1900 they erected a monument in Rochdale to local writers in the Lancashire dialect.

The age also manifested a reaction to the huge change in language attitudes that had emerged during the last quarter of the eighteenth century, and this proved to be of special importance for the contributors to *Punch*. The two decades between 1755 and 1775 were, to my mind, the most remarkable in the history of English. The first date saw the publication of Samuel Johnson's *A Dictionary of the English Language*, which went through four editions by 1773. In 1762 Bishop Robert Lowth published the first influential English grammatical textbook, *A Short Introduction to English Grammar*. And in 1774 John Walker presented his ideas for an English pronouncing dictionary that came to fruition in 1791. Suddenly, all three major domains of structure were being codified in a way that appealed to a class-conscious public, anxious to speak and write acceptably, and to avoid the social criticisms inherent in the refined 'polite' atmosphere of what has been called the 'century of manners'.

Pronunciation had a special appeal, compared to the usage issues that were being noticed in vocabulary and grammar. After all, if you are uncertain about the meaning or use of a particular word, you are going to encounter it only at intervals: how likely are you to encounter *disinterested* or *decimate* in everyday speech or writing? Similarly, if you are concerned about a point of grammatical usage, such as a split infinitive, it is not going to appear in every sentence. But pronunciation is never absent. Every word has to be pronounced. Every word has vowels and consonants. So pronunciation governs our intelligibility and identity, regional and social, more powerfully than any other aspect of spoken language. No wonder, then, that it attracted most attention from satirists. There are 387 items about language in the Victorian issues of *Punch*, and the largest group (96) deals with English pronunciation.

MR PUNCH TRIES TO HELP

During the first ten years of *Punch*, there is no mention of 'poor letter H'. The floodgates begin to open in 1852 (see p. 36). In this cartoon of 27 October 1855, Mr Punch gives polite advice to a Dickensian character. A decade later, the matter is dealt with more abruptly. In a short article entitled 'Vulgar Errors' (issue 47, 1864, p. 201), H heads the list, with double emphasis:

> It is a Vulgar Error, a very Vulgar Error, to omit or introduce improperly the letter H in conversation.

Mr Punch is thinking of sounds, of course, rather than letters, but in a pre-phonetics age this was the usual way of talking about pronunciation.

MR PUNCH TRIES TO HELP

'I beg your Pardon, Ma'am, but I think you dropped this?'

ELOCUTION WALKER

It took Walker fifteen years to complete his groundbreaking dictionary, and its success took him somewhat by surprise. He complains in the Advertisement to the Fourth Edition of 1806 how the rapid sale of the third had made him take up his pen again 'at a time of life, and in a state of health, little compatible with the drudgery and attention necessary for the execution of it'. He was right about the stress: he died a year later, aged 75.

The dictionary had over a hundred subsequent editions, and his name became a household word. Just as Johnson came to be called 'Dictionary Johnson', so Walker became known as 'Elocution Walker' – or just 'Walker'. Charles Dickens had no need to explain who Miss Blimber was talking about in chapter 14 of *Dombey and Son*, when she begins her analysis of the character of little Paul Dombey:

> 'If my recollection serves me,' said Miss Blimber breaking off, 'the word analysis as opposed to synthesis, is thus defined by Walker...'

Everyone would have known who Walker was, even though this was forty years after his death. In the twentieth century, a similar afterlife would be bestowed on 'Fowler'.

So what was it that made Walker's book so famous? The answer lies in its title, and in the further information that follows:

A CRITICAL
PRONOUNCING DICTIONARY
and EXPOSITOR *of the*
ENGLISH LANGUAGE

'Critical' was ambiguous. Walker was probably using it in the now obsolescent sense (as the *Oxford English Dictionary* defines it) of 'exercising careful judgement or observation'. But the judgemental sense of 'fault-finding' was also current in his day, and that certainly appears on the title-page:

RULES to be observed
by the Natives of SCOTLAND, IRELAND *and* LONDON
for avoiding their respective peculiarities

What did he mean?

JOHN WALKER (1802)

5

PROVINCIAL PECULIARITIES

By 'the natives of London', Walker was referring to working-class Cockneys, not the cultured and well-educated citizens of the capital. He describes London upper-class speech as 'the best' because it is 'more generally received' – he means received by cultured and educated society, who have taken their cue from the Court and other influential social institutions, such as the Church and the Universities. People look up to London because it is the capital city, he argues, and so it is important for its citizens to give a good impression to provincials, who lack the opportunities that the capital has to offer:

> [T]he great bulk of the nation, and those who form the most impor-
> tant part in it, are without these advantages, and therefore want such a
> guide to direct them as is here offered.

The further away they live, the worse their situation:

> [H]arsh as the sentence may seem, those at a considerable distance
> from the capital, do not only mispronounce many words taken
> separately, but they scarcely pronounce, with purity, a single word,
> syllable, or letter.

And that means the Scots and the Irish are in the worst danger of all, which is why they received special mention in the subtitle to his book.

In his preface, Walker has separate sections devoted to the 'peculiarities' of the Irish, the Scots (including a passing mention of the Welsh) and Cockney Londoners. He gives many examples, such as:

- The Irish should stop saying 'farum' for *farm* and 'helum' for *helm*.
- The Scots should stop lengthening their vowels, so that *vision* comes out as 'veesion' and *conscious* as 'cone-shus'.
- The Welsh should stop replacing voiced consonants with their voiceless counterparts, as when *big* is pronounced 'pick', *vice* as 'fice', and *jail* as 'chail'.

6

But most of his criticism is aimed at Cockneys, because their accent resides close to the Court and the City, and thus thrusts itself harshly into the ears of polite society. It may have fewer 'faults' than are found in provincial dialects, but it cannot be avoided. As a result:

> [T]he vulgar pronunciation of London, though not half so erroneous as that of Scotland, Ireland, or any of the provinces, is, to a person of correct taste, a thousand times more offensive and disgusting.

In fact, he identifies only four features:

- Cockneys pronounce *s* indistinctly after *st*, as in *posts* and *wastes*.
- They pronounce *w* for *v* and vice versa, as in the examples from Mr Weller (p. vii) – he calls it 'a blemish of the first magnitude'.
- They don't sound *h* after *w*, and thus confuse such pairs as *whales* and *Wales*.
- They don't sound *h* where it ought to be and vice versa: 'A still worse habit than the last prevails, chiefly among the people of London, that of sinking the h at the beginning of words where it ought to be sounded, and of sounding it, either where it is not seen, or where it ought to be sunk.'

Curiously, he makes no mention of the glottal stop, which was a really noticeable feature of Cockney speech then as now (as in *bo'le* for *bottle*). It is 'poor letter H' that gets most of the publicity.

POOR LETTER H

Tout Contractor (who has been paid a Shilling per Man, and sees his way to a little extra profit). 'Now, look 'ere, you Two H's! The Public don't want yer — nor *I* don't, nor Nobody don't; so jist Drop them Boards, and then 'ook it!'

14 *January 1865*

Mamma. 'Why Tom! What are you doing with that nasty Dust-pan and Broom?'

Tom. 'Brother Fred told me to bring it in and Sweep up all the H's Mɪs. Mopus had dropped about!' (*N.B. Great Expectations from Mrs. M.*)

16 May 1867

LETTER PERFECT

Cockney Pupil. 'Yes, Sir, goin' down to the Gov'nour's County-'Ouse —
'Ay-makin' an' that goin' on —'

Tutor. 'Ah, well, see and make a few H's as well, Mr. Pankridge, while you're
about it!'

3 August 1867

POOR LETTER H: UPSTAIRS & DOWNSTAIRS

During the Victorian era we see numerous booklets taking up this theme, such as *Poor Letter H, Its Use and Abuse: Addressed to its little vowels a, e, y, o, u, and the millions who use them*. This appeared in 1854, and sold 30,000 by the following year. No wonder it's such a big issue in the pages of *Punch*. And at the end of the century, when Punch anthologies were becoming very popular, virtually all the jokes at the expense of 'Arry and 'is friends in *Mr Punch's Cockney Humour* involve the *h*. But even the *Punch* writers were aware that things weren't so simple. At the very end of the collection we read:

> COCKNEY HOBSERVATION. Cockneys are not the only people who drop or exasperate the 'h's. It is done by common people in the provinces, and you may laugh at them for it. The deduction therefore is, that a peasant, with an 'h', is fair game.

However, the peasants weren't the only target. Anyone 'trying too hard' would be just as likely to appear in a *Punch* cartoon. Also 'fair game' were instances (to cultured ears) of ignorance – the auditorily blind leading the auditorily blind. H-clashes were commonplace when people from different classes met. And for some, following the norms of cultured pronunciation with respect to H was just too much effort.

CULTURE

Parlour-Maid (to Buttons). 'You Vulgar Boy! You should never say "Ax".
You should say "Harsk"!'

29 March 1884

TROP DE ZÈLE

(*An Aristocratic Tip*)

The New Companion (fresh from Girtham College). 'Yes, Lady Jane, I saw *H*er, with *H*er *H*abitual *H*ypocrisy *H*olding out *H*er *H*and to *H*im as *H*e was *H*aranguing at *H*is *H*otel —'

Lady Jane. 'Good gracious, Child, don't stick in your H's so carefully as all that! People will think your Father and Mother dropped 'em, and that you're tryin' to pick 'em up!' (*And People wouldn't be very far wrong.*)

11 June 1892

HI ART!

Parent. 'I should like you to be very Particular about his Hair.'

Photographic Artist (!). 'Oh, Mum, the 'air is heasy enough! It's the Hi's where we find the Difficulty!'

14

AN INCURABLE

Mamma. 'Algernon, you great silly Goose, I am ashamed of you! To get into such a state about that odious little Miss Griggs! Why, she was dropping her H's all over the room!'

Algernon. 'Was she? I only wish I'd known it; I'd have picked 'em up — and kept 'em!'

11 March 1865

15

'TWAS WHISPERED IN HEAVEN

(Hottest Day, Tuesday, July 14)

First Swell (languidly). 'How are you?'

Second Swell (still more languidly). ''Ot! Ve'y 'ot! Too great trouble to aspirate!'

25 July 1896

16

GOING TOO FAR

Things were clearly getting out of hand, according to Mr Walker Delolme, in a long letter to Mr Punch headed 'Un-English suggestion' (issue 90, 1886, p. 234), with the entire fabric of decent society at stake. Here's an extract:

> Democracy is indeed, in its own language, 'a going of it'. It has initiated a movement for the habitual omission from utterance of the letter 'H'. Yes, Sir, 'ARRY 'as 'is defenders. In a paper read before a Provincial Literary and Philosophical Society, to a popular audience, and since published, default of the aspirate is actually extenuated. Nay, its disuse is advocated even. From a London journal there is also quoted a 'plea' treating exactness in using it as a species of affectation. A notable point in one of these apologies is the theory that, as some people are partially colour-blind, so others may possibly be h-deaf-and-dumb; physically unable to hear or to pronounce the sound, h. Un'appy 'uman beings! 'Ow 'orrible! Why what is even 'Eaven with an 'H'? …
>
> Sir, I trust that the whole Constitutional Party, whether Liberals or Tories, will unite as one man in opposing an agitation opening a disloyal crusade against the Queen's English. Its commencement is clearly the thin end of the wedge, which, when driven home, will confound v and w, singular and plural, and deprive present participles of their final g, besides making the double negative compulsory – and that all in the sacred name of British liberty of speech!

THE DEMAND FOR ELOCUTION

Walker actually tried to be more inclusive in his treatment of pronunciation than those who had dealt with the subject before him. He writes:

> [I]f a solemn and familiar pronunciation really exists in our language, is it not the business of a grammarian to mark both?

He was thinking of Dr Johnson, in particular, who had been particularly worried about how to deal with this issue in his *Dictionary* (see p. 22). Johnson acknowledged that English had a 'double pronunciation; one, cursory and colloquial; the other, regular and solemn', but he gave up trying to handle the former, because of the way it was 'made different, in different mouths, by negligence, unskilfulness, or affectation'. It was, he famously wrote in his preface, like trying 'to enchain syllables, and to lash the wind'. And so he opted to present the solemn variety:

> For pronunciation the best general rule is, to consider those as the most elegant speakers who deviate least from the written words.

Follow the spelling. It's a principle that evolved during the Middle Ages, when an educated class, able to read and write, grew in numbers and influence. The question of whether words should begin with the letter H or not was one of the first to be noticed. The anonymous author of an early-fifteenth-century concordance to the Wycliffe Bible – the first known concordance to an English book – complains about it:

> [S]um man writeþ sum word wiþ an h, which saame word anoþir man writiþ wiþouten an h
>
> (A certain man writes a certain word with an *h*, which same word another man writes without an *h*.)

18

Clearly, the aspirate sound was often being dropped in everyday pronunciation, and it would only be when these words were being written down and widely read that speakers would begin to notice it.

And worry about it? There's no hint of any serious concern until the eighteenth century, when pronunciation came to be perceived as a critical faculty in presenting oneself in front of society. Lord Chesterfield, in one of his letters to his son, advised him to aim for 'an agreeable and distinct elocution; without which nobody will hear you with patience; this everybody may acquire, who is not born with some imperfection in the organs of speech'.

Elocution was the buzzword of the day. Thomas Sheridan, the father of the playwright, became famous for his lectures on elocution, speaking all over the country to packed halls. John Watkins, the editor of *Memoirs of Richard Brinsley Sheridan*, tells the story (p. 108):

> Mr. Sheridan was at this period busily engaged in delivering eight lectures on elocution, the subscription to which was one guinea for the course, with a ticket, entitling the bearer to a copy of the whole when published.* His reception was very flattering; and after reading his lectures to a crowded auditory at the west end of the town, he was prevailed upon to repeat them at Pewterer's Hall, in the city, and next at Spring Gardens. Incredible as it may seem, the fact is certain that he had upwards of sixteen hundred subscribers, at a guinea each, besides occasional visitors, which, with the advantage arising from the publication of the course, at half-a-guinea in boards, must have rendered his emoluments very considerable.

Indeed. Translating into modern values, that is equivalent to a course fee per person of about £75. One of his courses must have earned him well over £150,000 (in today's money).

---

* This would be *A Course of Lectures on Elocution* (1763).

JOHN WALKER (1732–1807)

THOMAS SHERIDAN (1719–1788)

FOLLOW THE SPELLING

The importance of correct spelling had also become an issue in the later eighteenth century, greatly fostered by the publication of Dr Johnson's *Dictionary* and the decisions he made. Johnson's aim had been to 'adjust' the orthography, 'which has been to this time unsettled and fortuitous', and many of his choices did indeed become standard.

The climate of the time is well illustrated by the statesman Lord Chesterfield, who wrote a series of letters to his son offering advice about correct behaviour. In his letter of 19 November 1750 he draws attention to the importance of correct spelling:

> I come now to another part of your letter, which is the orthography, if I may call bad spelling *orthography*. You spell induce, *enduce*; and grandeur, you spell grand*ure*; two faults, of which few of my house-maids would have been guilty. I must tell you, that orthography, in the true sense of the word, is so absolutely necessary for a man of letters, or a gentleman, that one false spelling may fix a ridicule upon him for the rest of his life; and I know a man of quality, who never recovered the ridicule of having spelled *wholesome* without the *w*.

Inevitably, spelling becomes a part of the H story.

PHILIP DORMER STANHOPE,
4TH EARL OF CHESTERFIELD (1694–1773)

THE ADVANTAGES OF EDUCATION

Small Boy. 'Look 'ere, Mawrd! I reckon the chap as keeps this shop ain't bin to school lately; 'e spells "*'all*" with a *haitch!*'

12 June 1901

24

SUPERIOR EDUCATION

Page Boy (to Jeames). 'Where shall I put thish 'er Dish of Ammonds?'

Jeames (with dignity). 'I'm surprised, Harthur, that at your Hage you 'aven't learnt 'ow to pernounce the *r* in Harmonds!'

9 January 1892

ONCE FOR ALL

Mistress. 'By the Way — Anna — Hannah — I'm not sure.
Is your Name "Anna" or "Hannah"?'

New Cook (tartly). 'Which my Name is Anna, Mum — Haich, Ha, Hen, Hen,
Ha, Haich, — "Anna".'

Mistress (giving it up in despair). 'Ah! Thank you.'

16 December 1871

26

Captain de Smith remonstrates with Mr. Holmes, the Vet of his Regiment, for mal-pronunciation of the word Horse — to him the Vet — 'Well, if a *H*atich, and a *H*o, and a *H*ar, and a *H*ess, and a *H*e, don't spell 'Orse — My name ain't 'Enery 'Omes!'

7 *March 1863*

SPELLING BEES

The *Oxford English Dictionary* has a first recorded usage of *spelling-bee* as 1875 – an event that took place at Myddelton Hall, Islington, London. Such events became very popular in the last quarter of the nineteenth century. Spelling was also a feature of school visits: any prominent person invited to address a class would invariably ask the children to spell out words – so much so that when asked a general knowledge question, it could take the class by surprise.

A CAPITAL ANSWER

'Self-made' Man (examining School, of which he is a Manager). 'Now, Boy, what's the capital of 'Olland?'

Boy. 'An "H", Sir.'

3 September 1870

Getting a spelling right, of course, depended on the questioner presenting a recognizable pronunciation – a point noted by the ever-observant Mr Punch.

A SPELLING B

As an independent test, Mr. Buttertub (Churchwarden and Overseer) is invited to put some questions.

Mr. B. 'Can any o' you Boys spell Tremenjeous?'!!

22 January 1876

COCKNEY VOWELS

Although the Cockney use of consonants attracted most of Mr Punch's satire, the distinctive vowels and diphthongs didn't escape. The pronunciation of 'ei' (as in *day*), 'oi' (as in *boil*) and 'ai' (as in *by*) seems to have been a regular source of confusion for speakers of RP.

CURIOSITIES OF CHOP-HOUSES

Gentleman. — 'Let's have a boiled mackerel.'

Waiter. — 'Biled, sir! Better have 'em briled, sir. If they're biled, they're spiled, sir!'

Issue 8, 1845

'Did yer order any Ile round the corner?'

'What do you mean by Ile? Do you mean Oil?'

'Naw. Not *Ile*, but *ILE* wot yer drinks!'

26 July 1899

POOR LETTER A

'Do you sell Type?' — 'Type, Sir? No, Sir. This is an Ironmonger's. You'll find Type at the Linendryper's over the w'y!'

'I don't mean *Tape*, Man! *Type*, for *Printing!*' — 'Oh, *Toype* yer mean! I beg yer pardon, Sir!'

18 December 1886

KEB, SIR?

In an article on the way London cab-drivers treat their customers, Mr Punch offers some friendly advice about pronunciation (issue 7, 1844, p. 46):

> In soliciting for employment, pronounce the word, cab, according to its orthography; that is, as it is spelt, c-a-b – cab, and not as if it were, k-e-b – keb. Your brethren almost invariably cry, 'Keb, sir!' 'Keb, sir!' There is no such word as keb in the English language; you annoy the correct ear exceedingly by using it; and besides, you set a bad example to youth, who learn to imitate the inaccuracy.

VOWEL WASHING

Mr Punch was never one to miss a fruitful pun, but many of his pronunciation jokes are unclear today, as we lack the relevant cultural background. This short article (issue 61, 1871, p. 110) is a case in point. With a bit of research, however, all becomes clear:

ALPHABETICAL INTELLIGENCE

What does this mean? It is an advertisement found in the *Times*:–

THE VOWEL WASHING MACHINE: its remarkable excellences – little water, little labour, little soap, great efficiency, great convenience, and great economy.

Why should we wash our vowels? How? with liquids? *i.e.*, wash *a, e, i, o, u*, and sometimes even *w* and *y*, with *l, m, n, r*.*

Who are employed in the work? Mutes? If so, it's a good time for the undertakers. But why not clean up our consonants a bit while we're about it? Surely The Vowel Washing Machine might be followed by the Aspirate Replacing Machine, for putting in H's where they were wanted, and (by a second movement) for taking them out when they were *de trop*. A Cockney friend, seeing this advertisement, observed, 'Well, I've 'eard of making 'a when the sun shines, but never of washing *a*.' So we left him; and we leave this to the consideration of our readers.

Hand-operated washing machines were introduced in the Great Exhibition of 1851, and began to be popular in the 1860s. Thomas Bradford of London and Manchester was the most famous manufacturer of the time, and his 'Victress Vowel' series was the most popular, produced in a number of different sizes to handle different workloads. The *Vowel E* model was designed for family use, *Vowel O* was larger and *Vowel U* was intended for very large institutions, such as hospitals and workhouses. His choice of name was a gift for Mr Punch.

---

* In Ben Jonson's *The English Grammar*, we see the first recorded use of *liquid* to refer to these consonants.

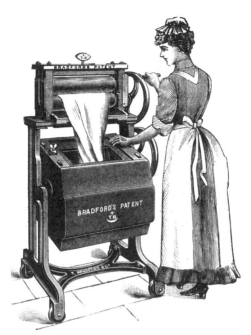

'Vowel' Washing-Machine

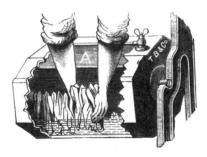

Placing Clothes in the 'Vowel' Washing-Machine

'VOWEL' WASHING MACHINE

Victress Vowel machine from Margaret Cuthbert Rankin, *The Art and Practice of Laundry Work.*

AMBIGUITIES

Punch writers made a great thing out of the supposed difficulties of understanding between the classes. The use of H was the main issue, but other sounds were also targets. A surprising number of word-pairs contrast in meaning through the use of an initial H.

ELUCIDATION!

Rector's Wife. 'How do you do, Mr. Wiggles? We have not seen you at Church lately! Have you been away?'

Mr. Wiggles. 'Yes, Mu'm, I've been a-visitin' my old 'Aunts at Manchester, Mu'm.'

Rector's Wife. 'Really! I hope you found the old Ladies quite well.'

Mr. Wiggles. 'I didn't say my Harnts, Mu'm — I said my old 'Aunts — revisitin' the 'Aunts o' my Youth, you know, Mu'm!'

22 November 1879

The distinction between *air* and *hair* received repeated attention, as in a short article headed 'Accidentally Correct' (issue 49, 1865, p. 246):

> The power of aspirating words, which Londoners are supposed to possess, but which provincials practise to an incalculably greater extent, sometimes hits the truth, though it is only by what is called a happy accident. For instance, we heard SLIPPER the other day, saying, 'The great fault he had to find with young ladies of the present day was, that they were always giving themselves such tremendously false *hairs.*' By Jove, he wasn't far wrong.

LETTER H

First Manly Voice. 'Beautiful Hair, isn't it, Fred?'

(*Laura, who had not expected to make a Conquest so soon as their first afternoon at Sludgey-on-the-Ooze, listens not displeased.*)

Second Manly Voice. 'Yes; — Nice Breeze, so Refreshin' after the 'eated Hatmosphere of the Metropolis!!'

(*And Laura was properly Chaffed by her Younger Sisters, who took stock of the Speakers.*)

13 August 1864

POOR LETTER H

'Have you got any *whole* Strawberry Jam?' — 'No, Miss. All ours is quite New!'

27 November 1886

ALARMING!

Hairdresser. 'They Say, Sir, the Cholera's in the *H*air, Sir!'

Gent., very uneasy. 'Indeed! Ahem! Then I Hope you're very Particular about the Brushes you use.'

Hairdresser. 'Oh! I see you don't *H*understand me, Sir. I don't mean the 'air of the 'ed, but the *H*air *h*of the *H*atomsphere!'

Issue 22, 1852

POSH PRONUNCIATION

Most of the pronunciation cartoons in Victorian *Punch* have regional speech as their targets; but upper-class habits aren't ignored. Three features recur: the habit of dropping the final -*g* in the -*ing* verb ending; the 'far back' pronunciation of words like *here* and *there*, with the last vowel sounding like 'aw'; and the substitution of /r/ by /w/. When these features combine, the result could evidently be unintelligible.

A SLIGHT MISUNDERSTANDING

'Do you evah *Wink*, Miss Evangeline?'

'Do I ever *what*, Mr. Smythe?'

'*Wink?*' — 'What *do* you mean, Sir?'

'Well, *Skate*, if you pwefer the Expression!'

6 November 1875

POOR LETTER G

The Duchess. 'Yes; Skatin' would be charmin', if it weren't for the Freezin' stoppin' the Huntin'!'

Lord Charles. 'Yes; and ain't Sleighin' toppin' fun, except for the Snowin' spoilin' the Skatin'!'

5 February 1887

41

PERSONAL INTEWEST

In issue 73 (1877, p. 119), there was a 62-line poetic protest by 'a Person of Quality'. The report was headed 'An Unpleasant Chapter of Auto-biography', and was introduced with the following words:

> In an address at the Athenaeum about human embryonic develop-ment, the speaker, Professor Thomson, referred to his audience's inevitable 'personal interest' in the topic. A report on the address commented: 'Each member of the British Association however noble his social lineage, and whatever noise he may make in the world now, can thus carry back his existence to that feeble spark of life which manifested itself in the merest speck of animal-jelly.'

The opening lines capture the thrust of the piece:

> 'Personal Intewest'? What atwocious wot!
> THOMSON's Addwess, a hcap of twivialities –
> *I* should have wather called a howwid lot
> Of wude, unintewesting personalities!
> This sort of thing is weally quite impwopah,
> And on all gentlemanly nerves must jar.
> It's time that somebody should put a stoppah
> 'On pushing pedigwees so pwecious far
> Into the wealms of Chaos and Old Night.'
> (A neat quotation that! I hope it's wight.)
> *Some* ancestwy is one of the essentials
> Of evewy person wanked above a Cad;
> But this pwepostewous fad
> For gwubbing among embwyos for cwedentials
> Of lengthy lineage is most disgusting,
> And wight-down wevolutionawy too;
> For, if there's any twusting
> These stowies – though *I* don't believe them twue –
> Who's to discwiminate 'twixt Cad and Swell? He

42

Who's in the purple born has little pull
Over the Snob, with empty purse or full,
If both date back to a mere speck of jelly!

A PUZZLE

Scene — Village Inn, Hampshire.

Languid Swell. "Sthawa Wifl'caw heaw?'

Barmaid. "Beg Pard'n, Sir!'

Swell. "Sthawa Wifl'caw heaw?"

Barmaid. 'Don't understand French, Sir!'

Swell. 'Haw!' (*Exit.*)

(*He is supposed to have meant*, 'Is there a Rifle Corps here?')

20 May 1876

43

SCOTS PRONUNCIATION

Mr Punch evidently found the Scots accent unintelligible, and expressed some surprise that the inhabitants of Scotland could actually understand each other – albeit with difficulty sometimes.

THE RETURN OF THE NATIVE

Tam. 'Sae ye've gotten back, Sanders?'

Sanders. ''Deed, aye. I've just gotten back.'

Jamie. 'An' hoo did 'e like London?'

Sanders. 'Od, it's an outlandish place yon! They tell't me they couldna unnerstaun ma Awccent!'

John. 'Awccent! I never heard tell that Fife folk had *ony* Awccent!'

28 September 1895

44

'THE QUEEN'S ENGLISH' (OR SCOTCH)

Minister. 'Weel, John, an hoo did ye like ma Son's discoorse?'

John. 'Weel, Meenister, ah maun admeet he's vera Soond, but, oh Man! he's no Deep! His Pronoonciation's no vera gweed; but ah've nae doobt he'll impruv'!'

4 February 1882

45

THE WH- PROBLEM

Although Walker had recommended the 'voiceless w' in words like *whales* and *wheel*, it was soon dropped by speakers of RP, who probably found it too Celtic for their liking – it was a feature of Irish, Welsh and Scots accents. Certainly, by the turn of the century, the stage was set for a breakdown in communication of the kind reported in this dramatized account (issue 119, 1900, p. 211).

Anyone unfamiliar with the early history of bicycle manufacture will need to know that the first major commercialization of the free wheel had taken place in Germany just two years before, and was beginning to catch on everywhere. Previously, there had been only a fixed wheel – the pedals revolving when the wheels do. Today we free-wheel without thinking about it, but the option was evidently controversial when the new technology first arrived:

THE ENGLISH ACCENT

SCENE – Lady TRANKERTON's *dinner-party.* LORNA T., *daughter of the house, twenty and athletic, sits next to Professor* ANDREW McFIDDLE, D.D., *of Glasgow University, rather deaf and very Scotch.*

Lorna. (after trying various other topics unsuccessfully). I wonder if you take any interest in the free-wheel controversy, Professor.

Prof. McF. (starting). The free weel controversy? (*Aside*) What are our weemen-folk coming to! It's amazing! (*Aloud*) My dear young lady, it has been the work of my life to study that controversy in all its arspects.

Lorna. No, really? How *interesting*! I had no idea – (*Aside*) Fancy, an old fossil like that! But of course everyone does it nowadays. (*Aloud*) And do you believe in the free-wheel?

Prof. McF. It is a deeficult question. Furrst you must define what you mean by a free weel.

Lorna. (*aside*). How horribly Scotch! (*Aloud*) Oh, the ordinary make, you know.

Prof. McF. (*aside*). The flippancy of these English lassies! (*Aloud, sternly*) If you mean the ordinary *conception*, it simply does not exeest.

Lorna. Oh, but I've got one, and so has TED.

Prof. McF. A common delusion! Are you not aware that all action is governed by a motive or motives?

Lorna. Ye-es – of course. (*Aside*) Good gracious! If he's going to talk mechanics I'm done for. (*Aloud*) But really, Professor, I didn't think you were going to drag me into such philosophical depths over an argument on a cycle.

Prof. McF. (*aside*). Argument in a circle? The brazen hussy! (*Aloud*) It is no such thing. If you will show me the flaw in the argument I shall be *obliged* to you.

Lorna. (*aside*). He seems very testy. (*Aloud*) No, you misunderstand me. Of course, after all these years of study you must know. Only, I *can't* help believing in my own free-wheel.

Prof. McF. (propitiated). It is natural. Until you realise that effect follows cause and action motive.

Lorna. (*with temerity*). Yes, but isn't the whole *idea* of the free-wheel that the action is *independent* of the motive?

Prof. McF. That is the common idea, undoubtedly, and it is as absurd as it is false. But for motive there would be no moral character attaching to action.

Lorna. (*aside*). What *can* he be driving at now? (*Aloud*) I'm afraid, if you're going to discuss the morals of bicycling –

Prof. McF. Of what? I am a little deaf on this side. The morals of what?

Lorna. (*loudly*). Bicycling. [*Awful pause*]

Prof. McF. (*eyeing her severely*). Are we discussing the free weel or the bicycle?

Lorna. Why – both. The – the free-wheel *is* a bicycle, isn't it?

Prof. McF. (after consuming the savoury in silence). It occurs to me, Miss TRANKERTON, that there is just a possibeelity that you have been talking of a trifling mechanical invention known as the free *h*weel.

Lorna. (thoroughly mystified). Of course. Haven't you?

Prof. McF. Certainly not. I have been endeavouring to hold a rational conversation on the metapheesical subject of the free *weel. In Scotland, we do not drop our h's.*

Lorna. (to herself, in the night watches). Oh! why didn't I say, 'In England we don't strain our I's?'

THE 'IRREPRESSIBLE' AGAIN

Gent in Knickerbockers. 'Rummy Speakers them 'Ighlanders, 'Enery. When we wos Talking to one of the 'Ands, did you Notice 'im saying "*Nozzing*" for "*Nothink*", and "*She*" for "'*E*"?'

12 October 1872

Today we associate knickerbockers with children's wear, but they were fashionable among adults in the second half of the nineteenth century – for men, loose-fitting breeches, gathered in at the knee and worn especially by sportsmen and travellers.

JOHNSON AND BOSWELL

A satirical engraving of Johnson having tea with Boswell and his wife in Edinburgh in 1773. It was etched in 1786 by Thomas Rowlandson after a sketch by Samuel Collings.

DR JOHNSON ON THE SCOTS ACCENT

In chapter 24 of his *Life of Johnson*, James Boswell (1740–1795) records the conversation when he introduced Johnson to the Scottish gentleman Sir Alexander Macdonald in 1772 (here shown with some paragraph divisions added, for ease of reading):

SIR A.: I have been correcting several Scotch accents in my friend Boswell. I doubt, sir, if any Scotchman ever attains to a perfect English pronunciation.

JOHNSON: Why, sir, few of them do, because they do not persevere after acquiring a certain degree of it. But, sir, there can be no doubt that they may attain to a perfect English pronunciation, if they will. We find how near they come to it; and certainly a man who conquers nineteen parts of the Scottish accent, may conquer the twentieth.

But, sir, when a man has got the better of nine-tenths he grows weary, he relaxes his diligence, he finds he has corrected his accent so far as not to be disagreeable, and he no longer desires his friends to tell him when he is wrong; nor does he choose to be told. Sir, when people watch me narrowly, and I do not watch myself, they will find me out to be of a particular county. In the same manner, Dunning [Lord Ashburton] may be found out to be a Devonshire man. So most Scotchmen may be found out. But, sir, little aberrations are of no disadvantage. I never catched Mallet in a Scotch accent; and yet Mallet, I suppose, was past five-and-twenty before he came to London.

INOFFENSIVE BOSWELL

Judging by this next account, Boswell evidently was unsure about his own accent. James Love was an actor-manager that Boswell had first met in Edinburgh. 'Old Mr Sheridan' was Thomas Sheridan, whose elocution courses are referred to on p. 19:

> Upon another occasion I talked to him on this subject, having myself taken some pains to improve my pronunciation, by the aid of the late Mr. Love, of Drury Lane Theatre, when he was a player at Edinburgh, and also of old Mr. Sheridan. Johnson said to me, 'Sir, your pronunciation is not offensive.' With this concession I was pretty well satisfied; and let me give my countrymen of North Britain an advice not to aim at absolute perfection in this respect; not to speak *High English*, as we are apt to call what is far removed from the *Scotch*, but which is by no means *good English*, and makes 'the fools who use it' truly ridiculous.
>
> Good English is plain, easy, and smooth in the mouth of an unaffected English gentleman. A studied and facetious pronunciation, which requires perpetual attention, and imposes perpetual constraint, is exceedingly disgusting. A small intermixture of provincial peculiarities may perhaps have an agreeable effect, as the notes of different birds concur in the harmony of the grove, and please more than if they were all exactly alike.
>
> I could name some gentlemen of Ireland to whom a slight proportion of the accent and recitative of that country is an advantage. The same observation will apply to the gentlemen of Scotland. I do not mean that we should speak as broad as a certain prosperous member of Parliament from that country [the Lord Advocate, Mr Dundas]; though it has been well observed that it has been of no small use to him, as it rouses the attention of the House by its uncommonness, and is equal to tropes and figures in a good English speaker.
>
> I would give as an instance of what I mean to recommend to my countrymen, the pronunciation of the late Sir Gilbert Elliot; and may I presume to add that of the present Earl of Marchmont, who told me,

with great good humour, that the master of a shop in London, where he was not known, said to him, 'I suppose, sir, you are an American!' 'Why so, sir?' said his lordship. 'Because, sir,' replied the shopkeeper, 'you speak neither English nor Scotch, but something different from both, which I conclude is the language of America.'

At another point, Boswell and Johnson discuss pronunciation dictionaries. Johnson is not especially enamoured of them. Sheridan's dictionary was published in 1780:

BOSWELL It may be of use, sir, to have a Dictionary to ascertain pronunciation.

JOHNSON Why, sir, my Dictionary shows you the accent of words, if you can but remember them.

BOSWELL But, sir, we want marks to ascertain the pronunciation of the vowels. Sheridan, I believe, has finished such a work.

JOHNSON Why, sir, consider how much easier it is to learn a language by the ear than by any marks. Sheridan's Dictionary may do very well, but you cannot always carry it about with you; and when you want the word, you have not the Dictionary. It is like a man who has a sword that will not draw. It is an admirable sword, to be sure; but while your enemy is cutting your throat, you are unable to use it.

Besides, sir, what entitles Sheridan to fix the pronunciation of English? He has, in the first place, the disadvantage of being an Irishman; and if he says he will fix it after the example of the best company, why, they differ among themselves. I remember an instance: when I published the plan for my Dictionary, Lord Chesterfield told me that the word *great* should be pronounced so as to rhyme with *state*; and Sir William Yonge sent me word that it should be pronounced so as to rhyme with *seat*, and that none but an Irishman would pronounce it *grait*. Now here were two men of the highest rank, the one the best speaker in the House of Lords, the other the best speaker in the House of Commons, differing entirely.

Ambiguities multiplied when people travelled around the country and encountered other accents. Mr Punch was especially interested in what happened when the Cockneys met the Scots: two completely different accents could result in the same set of sounds being used for two different words, as the cartoon on p. 55 shows. *Ale* for a Cockney would sound like *isle*. In the Scots accent shown, *oil* also sounded like *isle*. Result: total confusion.

Presumably the barrister in the cartoon on p. 56 had a cultured accent of some kind, so that his pronunciation of the first syllable in *diary* overlapped with the Scots lady's pronunciation of the first syllable in *dairy*.

ANOTHER MISUNDERSTANDING

'Arry (on a Northern Tour, with Cockney pronunciation). 'Then I'll 'ave a Bottle of Aile.'

Hostess of the Village Inn. '*Ile*, Sir? We've nane in the hoose, but Castor Ile or Paraffine. Wad only o' them dae, Sir?'

22 June 1895

A PROMISING WITNESS!

Scotch Counsel (addressing an Old Woman in a case before Judge and Jury).
'Pray, my good Woman, do you keep a Diary?'

Witness. 'Naw, Sir, I kups a Whuskey Shop!'

9 September 1893

PRONOUNCING PLACE-NAMES

Nothing seems to have riled Mr Punch more than the way place-names were being called out on buses and trains. The magazine had barely been out a year when it began to take omnibus conductors to task for their pronunciation of local names. In an article titled 'The omnibus cad's vocabulary, or, the idioms of conductors, done into English' (issue 2, 1842, p. 35), we read of such local pronunciations as 'Helephant', 'Hangel', 'Ngton' (for both Paddington and Islington), 'Mpton' (Brompton), 'Nich' (Greenwich), 'Wich' (Woolwich) and 'Smith' (Hammersmith).

Over the next decade, there were evidently some improvements – Mr Punch himself taking the credit – but not enough. A long article (issue 33, 1857, p. 57) pointed out the continuing dangers, and suggested a solution:

REFORM YOUR RAILWAY CALLS

We lately noticed the extreme economy of speech which is practised upon most, if not on all our Railroads, on the part of those officials whose vocation it is to shout out to every train that stops there the name of the respective station at which they are stationed. As hints thrown out in *Punch* are invariably acted on, it is no surprise to us to find that at the places which we instanced, there has been since our remonstrance, a decidedly more liberal supply of language. We have more than once been gratified by hearing the entire pronunciation of 'New Cross', and twice at least we have been treated with the missing syllables which expand the abbreviated ''Nam' into 'Sydenham'. The spirit of improvement, too, appears to be infectious, and its effects are evidently spreading to adjacent stations. A month ago we never should have dreamt of hearing anything but 'Nor' when our train pulled up at Norwood, but yesterday we heard the word in its complete dissyllability; and this very afternoon we have positively had no less than thirteen hairs turned grey, by the shock of joy it gave us to hear the proper aspirate prefixed to 'Forest 'ill', a feat that not the oldest passenger can, we fancy, call to mind that he has ever heard accomplished.

We trust that this example will be generally followed, and that on all our railways the process of articulation will be more attended to. Even on the Eastern Counties there is room for some reform in this respect at least, if not in any other. We were lately travellers on this delightful line, and the tediousness of our journey was most pleasantly beguiled by the excitement of endeavouring, when we reached a station, to recognise the name of it in what we heard bawled out to us. In the first thirty miles of Eastern Counties travelling there are no less than four stopping stations having names of two syllables, the last of which is 'ford': and as the prefix Strat-, Il-, Chelms-, or Rom-, is very rarely audible, a nervous passenger is kept in an unceasingly excited state, lest in this quartette of 'fords' he should be carried past the right one, the chances being three to one at least in favour of his being so. ...

We suggest that every railway should start an elocution class, which every station-caller engaged upon the line should, once a week at least, be expected to attend. Moreover, it might be as well to have some special auditors of stations' names appointed, whose duty it should be to travel up and down the line, and weekly certify that every one employed had been attentive to his calling.

Should these not prove sufficient means to ensure in Railway calls a more distinct articulation, we would recommend that the utterance of clipped words which will not pass as current English should in future be considered an indictable offence; and that, if needful, a special Act of Parliament be passed by which this wilful mutilation of the language may be punished. ... From hearing such continual contractions of speech, a passenger might almost fancy that the calling out at stations was a work performed by contract; but as this is not the case, we see no reason why these speech-contractors should not be compelled to furnish a more liberal supply of syllables. As it is, one really cannot go a dozen miles by rail without hearing a good deal of what in its curtailment may be called bad language; and although our better nature may instinctively recoil from the unenlightened principle of giving tit for tat, still we cannot help suggesting that officials must expect to be called names themselves, if they will not take the pains to call names more distinctly.

EN PASSANT

'Rather remarkable, ain't it, Sir? But 'ave you hever noticed as mostly all the Places on this Line begins with a "H"?'

'Aw — 'beg your Pardon?'

'Look at 'em! — 'Ampstead, 'Ighgate, 'Ackney, 'Omerton, 'Endon, 'Arrow, 'Olloway, and 'Ornsey!'

25 March 1876

UNDERGROUND PRONUNCIATIONS

The London Underground began in 1863. It was not long before Mr Punch noted the same malaise and reiterated his solution:

INARTICULATE INFORMATION

It is highly requisite that the Directors of the Underground Railway should cause those servants of theirs whose duty it is to call out the names of the stations to be taught to speak intelligibly. The eye often misses the station's name as the train passes it. You'll hear a fellow shouting "Oosh! 'Oosh!' for example, or 'N'il! N'il!' What can you make out of Nil, but nothing; and what more can you understand from 'Oosh? He means 'Shepherd's Bush', and 'Notting Hill'. It would be good of Mr. MACREADY to come out of his retirement and give those inarticulate railway men lessons on elocution.*

Whilst on this subject we may also observe that the conductors of certain omnibuses are in the habit of uttering a cry which may sometimes occasion gross misapprehension. As they go, or halt, on their journey westward, they keep continually calling out 'EMMA SMITH! EMMA SMITH!' Who is EMMA SMITH? a country gentleman might ask. They are supposed to mean Hammersmith. (issue 54, 1868, p. 73)

A year later (issue 57, 1869, p. 44), even the Cockneys were getting upset:

BY OUR COCKNEY

... what a nice line the Great Northern to Hedgeware is, to be sure. I am, as you know, werry partikler about my 'H"s, but "ang me', as my friend 'ARRY BELVILLE says, 'if t'ain't enough to spoil your pronunshiashun for a Hage and Hall time to 'ave to 'ear such names of stations one atop o' t'other, as the followin' as called out by the porters an' guards.'

---

* The actor William Macready (1793–1873) had retired from the stage after a farewell performance of *Macbeth* at Drury Lane on 26 February 1851.

’Olloway.
Seven Scissors Road.
Crouch Hend.
’Ighgate and ’Ampstead.
Heast Hend.
Finchley and ’Endon.
Mill ’Ill.
Hedgeware.

There’s a lot for you! And t’other line goes to Arford, Atfield, and Saint All-buns.

AGAIN!

First Gent. ’’Eard about the Sea-Serpent they’ve caught at Oban?’

Second Ditto. ‘Sea-Serpent caught in ’Olborn! ’Must be an ’Oax!!’

26 May 1877

61

DIAGNOSIS

'I can tell you what *you're* suffering from, my good Fellow! You're suffering from *Acne!*'

'*'Ackney?* Why, that's just what *t'other* Medical Gent he told me! *I only wish I'd never been near the Place!*'

23 January 1875

LAW AND LINDLEY MURRAY

This article appeared in Punch issue 27 (1854, p. 7). The title is somewhat misleading. The writer is remembering the author of *English Grammar*, which was published in 1795. By 1854 it had sold around 2 million copies, and sales continued until the last decade of the nineteenth century. But Murray's book was largely about parts of speech and syntax. Pronunciation does receive some treatment, towards the end of the book, but chiefly in relation to such matters as word-stress and prosody, and not the kind of vowel substitutions that have ended up here in court. A more apposite title would have been 'Law and John Walker' (p. 4):

> It is generally thought that the precedent set by one of our most distinguished English Judges, in not only giving judgement upon the merits of a case tried before him, but in deciding upon the right pronunciation of a word used in the pleadings, has given great satisfaction. A series of cases has since been heard, in which various offenders against the laws of language have been amerced in divers penalties. The following is a report of Saturday's sittings:–
>
> #### COURT OF QUEEN'S BENCH
> LORD CAMPBELL, at three o'clock, said that the paper having now been gone through, he and his brothers were ready to take any cases of bad language.
>
> Several barristers immediately left the Court. It was observed that some of them were gentlemen who had obtained notoriety by abusing unfortunate coroners and other magistrates of limited powers of committal.
>
> #### THE QUEEN V. LORD JOHN RUSSELL.
> The defendant was charged with habitually offending against HER MAJESTY'S English, by making a noise sounding like 'obleege', when he was supposed to intend to say 'oblige'.
>
> The defendant pleaded guilty, but urged that a hundred years ago his pronunciation was the fashionable one. It was derived from the French.

Lord Campbell said, that in the case of John Kemble *v.* the Prince Regent the *dictum* had been, 'It would become your Royal mouth better to say "oblige".' The rule was clear. Had the defendant anything further to say?

The defendant said that he had once visited the Lyceum Theatre, and had heard Mr. Frank Matthews say, in a burlesque called *Robin Hood* –

'With any advice about the siege,
The Field-Marshal therefore cannot obleege.'

Lord Campbell said that this proved that the defendant had been warned. The object of burlesque – and he was bound to say that such object was usually attained – was to ridicule what was absurd, by pushing absurdity to the extreme. The Court did not desire to be hard upon the defendant. Would he undertake not to repeat the offence?

The defendant said that he would endeavour to conform to the customs of the day; but he believed that in Magna Charta –

He was here somewhat hastily removed from the Court.

THE QUEEN V. RICHARD CORDEN.

The defendant was charged with laying a false emphasis upon the third syllable in the word inimical, which he pronounced inim*i*cal.

The defendant said that he had not intended to give offence, and that he had heard the same pronunciation from the Treasury Bench last week.

Lord Campbell said that the Treasury had better go to its 'Tyronis [beginner's] *Thesaurus*'. (*Laughter, in which nobody joined.*) The pronunciation was pedantic – why did not the defendant say sever-*i*ty and urban*i*ty?

The defendant was discharged with a caution.

THE QUEEN V. THIRTEEN CABMEN.

The defendants were charged with having said they were going to drive to the Adelphi Theáter.

The police gave evidence that this abominable pronunciation was of common occurrence, and gave great annoyance to the aristocratic classes on their way to the opera.

The defendants said that it was the ordinary pronunciation of the trading and lower orders.

Lord Campbell said that it was intolerable, and sentenced the whole of the defendants to be civil to their fares for an entire month.

The defendants were removed, one of them remarking that the sentence would be the death of him.

THE QUEEN V. THE HON. ALFRED LAZYTONGS.

The defendant was charged with having used continuous bad language through a whole afternoon, at the Conservative Club. He was proved to have said that the rain was a baw, that Mademoiselle Luther was a charming creechaw, the Lord Derby had come out strong about Canadaw, and that his, defendant's, tigaw was a deuced sharp little fellow.

Several old members of the club pressed for a severe punishment, as they said the offence was so common as to render the place quite unbearable. The young fellows went lounging about in their all-round collars, gobbling out the most ridiculous sounds, and fancying they were talking.

The defendant hoped that the Court would think it didn't mattaw what a parcel of red-faced old pumps thought on the subject.

Lord Campbell said that extraneous matter had been imported into the case on both sides. The Court had no jurisdiction over collars or red faces. But the defendant stood self-convicted. What had he to say?

The defendant said that a gentleman liked to speak differently from vulgarians, and as the latter clipped the Queen's English upon all occasions, it was the duty of a loyal subject to make as much of it as possible.

Lord Campbell said that the defence was plausible, but would not do. The proper way for a gentleman to render his language different from that of vulgarians was to take care that it was precise and accurate, and the vehicle for good sense or true wit. As the defendant seemed desirous to do what was right, he would accept his own bail for his reappearance that day month, conditionally on his reading *Punch* for one hour every day, during the intermediate time.

The defendant gladly gave this undertaking, and was discharged.

One thing leads to another in the exchange in the cartoon below. The misunderstanding begins with H, and is compounded by a problem of word division. The contrast between *bird's tail* and *bird stale* isn't actually a matter of accent at all: the ambiguity could equally have arisen in RP, where it's often a source of playfulness, as in 'I scream for ice-cream'.

Cook (to young Mistress, who has received a present of some game).
'And, please'm, do you like the birds 'igh?'

Mistress (puzzled). 'The bird's eye?'

Cook. 'What I mean, Mum, is, some prefers the birds stale.'

Mistress (more puzzled). 'The tail?' (*Decides not to seem ignorant.*) 'Send up the bird, please, Cook, with the eyes *and* the tail!'

13 March 1901

66

By all accounts, the two diphthongs heard in such words as *know* caused especial problems. Cockneys pronounced this with a more open onset – as they still do today – so that, to speakers of RP (p. vii), *know* would sound like *now*. The railway clerk in the cartoon below evidently had or affected the upper-class accent.

'Arriet. 'Wot toime his the next Troine fer 'Ammersmith?'

Clerk. 'Due now.'

'Arriet. ''Course Oi dawn't now, Stoopid, or I wouldn't be harskin' yer!'

11 July 1900

PRONOUNCING SURNAMES

There's no law governing the way we spell or pronounce our names. Most people are happy to use a spelling that transparently reflects the pronunciation, otherwise they face a lifetime of spelling out their name to others and correcting someone's mispronunciation of it. On the other hand, if you want to be different, by adopting a fanciful spelling or an unpredictable pronunciation, you may do as you wish; and especially during the sixteenth and seventeenth centuries, if you were a member of high society, it was a fashion statement to be orthographically idiosyncratic. Your preferences were recognized, and to address people wrongly would immediately show that you did not belong to their class – a serious social faux pas for the rising middle class of the eighteenth and nineteenth centuries.

The most extreme forms of naming eccentricity developed in upper-class families anxious to distinguish themselves from the same surname used by the lower classes, as when Featherstonhaugh – a quite common surname in the north of England, derived from a place-name – came to be pronounced 'Fanshaw'. Mr Punch evidently had lost patience with such affectations, and proposes a legal solution (issue 6, 1844, p. 215):

ACT FOR THE AMENDMENT OF
THE ORTHOGRAPHY OF SURNAMES

Whereas divers and sundry persons, subjects of Her Most Gracious Majesty, Victoria, of Great Britain and Ireland Queen, Defender of the Faith, are known, called, and designated by certain surnames, which are spelt one way and pronounced another; and whereas such names are so spelt that nobody upon earth could, from their spelling, have the remotest idea of their pronunciation; by reason whereof, others, faithful subjects of Her said Majesty, are continually led into mistakes in the utterance of them, thereby often giving offence to their owners, and exposing themselves unto derision and ridicule, to their no small discomfort and discomposure of mind; and moreover whereas a great many other inconveniences are by the same means occasioned;

BE IT ENACTED, That from the passing of this Act, henceforth and for ever, no Person calling himself CHUMLEY shall spell his name CHOLMONDELY; and that all manner of Persons who think proper to spell their names CHOLMONDELY, shall pronounce their said names, and have them pronounced of others, precisely as they are spelt; that is to say, as words of four syllables, with a due and distinct emphasis on each.

AND WHEREAS the name of BEAUCHAMP is of French origin, be it further enacted, that the said name shall be sounded of all men as nearly as possible after the French manner, and shall not be pronounced BEECHAM under any pretence whatever; and that all manner of Persons calling themselves BEECHAM shall write and spell their names, and shall have them written and spelt accordingly; provided always, that in case they prefer to spell them BEECHUM, they shall be at liberty to do so.

In like manner, BE IT FURTHER ENACTED, That MARJORIBANKS shall be spelt MARCHBANKS; WEMYS, WIMS; and COLQUHOUN, COHOON; or if not, then that they also shall be pronounced as they are spelt, and not in any other manner. And furthermore, BE IT ENACTED, That all other names not expressly mentioned in this Act shall be spoken according to their orthography. And lastly, BE IT ENACTED, That any person, of what degree soever, offending against any one of the provisions of this Act, either by spelling his own name, or that of any body else, differently from the way in which he pronounces it, or, by pronouncing it differently from the manner in which he spells it, shall forfeit for each offence a sum not exceeding Five Shillings.

Mr Punch comments:

> If the above Bill is not likely to do as much good to the country as any that has been as yet introduced into Parliament this session, *Punch* will allow himself to be shot.

Having failed in this initiative, some years later he hits on a poetic solution (issue 64, 1873, p. 165):

POETRY AND PROPER NAMES

(The former assisting you to pronounce the latter)

They dwelt an old cobbler at Bromley,
And he had a daughter so comely,
That, though he was poor,
And SNOOKS for name bore,
That name she relinquished for CHOLMONDELEY.

A small barber shaved for a penny;
His shop was the pride of Kilkenny.
He hung out his pole
Along with a scroll,
Whereon was inscribed ABERGAVENNY.

A school was for boys kept at E'sham,
By one who knew not how to teach 'em;
Yet his line he could trace
To a generous race.
This poor pedagogue called himself BEAUCHAMP.

There is choice of a great many large banks,
For those with their money who charge banks.
And one I would trust
With the whole of my 'dust',
Need I say, it is yours MESSRS. MARJORIBANKS.

A soldier may genius or dunce be;
But either can slain only once be.
As one was whose name
Is worthy of fame;
That hero of Waterloo, PONSONBY.

ACTORS' PRONUNCIATION

In Act 3 Scene 2 of *Hamlet*, the prince gives some advice to the players who visit him at Elsinore:

> Speak the speech, I pray you, as I pronounced it to you, trippingly on the tongue: but if you mouth it, as many of your players do, I had as lief the town-crier spoke my lines.

Evidently this advice was being ignored on the Victorian stage, where the town crier's habit of over-articulation seems to have been the norm. Mr Punch couldn't stand it (issue 8, 1845, p. 150):

INTERROGATORIES FOR PLAYERS

What do actors and actresses mean by saying, 'Skee-yi', 'Blee-yew', 'Kee-yind', and 'Dis-gyee-ise', for Sky, Blue, Kind, and Disguise? Are the ladies and gentlemen in question aware that all those words are words of one syllable, except the last, which has two, and of which they make three! Are they ignorant of these facts, or do they think it fine or elegant thus to tamper with the QUEEN's English? If they do, let PUNCH seriously assure them that they are mistaken; he very much wishes that they would break themselves of this habit, which he can never go to a theatre without being annoyed by. Especially has he to complain of certain 'Walking Gentlemen'; to whom he would feel greatly obliged if they would pay a little more attention to their Walker.

A 'walking gentleman'? The term is first recorded in 1794, referring to a male actor playing a small part with little or no speech. We would call them 'spear-carriers' today.

His strictures evidently had no effect, for a few years later we see him returning to the same theme, at much greater length (issue 24, 1853, p. 33):

... there is a peculiar spell about the stage, which is only to be met with in the pronunciation of those who appear before a theatrical audience. ... We should like to ask ... why it is that the orthography of real life is abandoned on the other side of the footlights.

We would ask why the letter *t* can't be followed in the same word by the letter *r* without the intrusion of an impertinent vowel to disturb the union? Why in fact is 'retribution' always 'rctc-ribution' in the mouth of the tragedian? and why cannot he utter the word 'truth' without putting into it so many eeee's as to make it a matter of much difficulty, and no ease at all to follow him? The letter *r* altogether seems to be marked out for persecution on the stage, as even at the beginning or the end of a word it is not allowed to have its natural force, without an attempt to tack something extraneous on to it. For example, 'revenge' is sure to become 'a-a-revenge' in the ordinary actor's mouth, and 'terror' is amplified into 'terror-a' by the lips of the 'leading man' at a melo-dramatic establishment.

The treatment of the vowels is often no less cruel than that of the consonants, and a system of substitution is practised with no other apparent motive than to make speaking on the stage as unlike speaking anywhere else as possible. ... 'Terrible' is converted into 'terra-bul'; a 'crime' is rendered far more atrocious by being extended into a 'cer-r-r-r-ime'; and the actor generally makes an injudicious display of his love of letters, by dragging as many letters as he can into every syllable he utters. We hear occasionally of youth having been driven to the theatre by certain aspirations, and, indeed, those aspirations have often been manifest to the audience; though they have been sadly misplaced, for what can justify the aspiration which converts 'action' into 'haction', and treats 'every hope of earthly happiness' as nothing better than 'hevery ope of hearthly appiness'. We should be very glad to break the disenchantment of the sort of spell that hovers about the atmosphere of the stage; and, if we have spoken plainly, it is only with the hope that the actors may attempt to follow the example, by trying to speak for the future as plainly as we have done.

Actors weren't the only culprits. Singers offended Mr Punch as well…

POOR LETTER 'O'

Signor Mossini. 'Ow, my Love! I loved her sow!
My Love that loved me years agow!'

AMERICAN PRONUNCIATION

An unexpected development in the last quarter of the nineteenth century was the emergence of American English as an admired variety in English high society. Mr Punch had regularly complained about the American words that were entering English in increasing numbers, such as *recuperate* and *burgle*. He wasn't alone. Henry Alford, the Dean of Canterbury Cathedral, is especially scathing in his book *A Plea for the Queen's English* (1860), complaining about 'the process of deterioration which our Queen's English has undergone at the hands of the Americans'. But after the Civil War, the combined effects of American economic growth, international influence and faster transportation altered the cultural climate. American writers, such as Ralph Waldo Emerson, Mark Twain and Artemus Ward (who contributed to *Punch*), made hugely popular lecture tours in Britain, and gave American English a fresh appeal, as the cartoon on p. 75 illustrates.

THE NEW SOCIETY CRAZE

The New Governess (through her pretty nose). 'Waall — I come right slick away from Ne'York City, an' I ain't had much time for foolin' around in Europe — you bet! So I can't fix up your Gals in the Eu-rôpean Languages, no-how!'

Belgravian Mamma (who knows there's a Duke or two still left in the Matrimonial Market). 'Oh, that's of no consequence. I want my Daughters to acquire the American accent in all its purity — and the Idioms, and all that. Now I'm sure *you* will do *admirably*!'

1 December 1888

TAKING COCKNEY SERIOUSLY?

John Walker is placed on a pedestal at the top of an article headed 'On the Cockney pronunciation' (issue 4, 1843, p. 169). It was written by an anonymous philologist, apparently born and bred in London, who seemed to be justifying the most noticeable features of Cockney pronunciation. Walker had been dead for thirty-five years, but general awareness of his stature was still taken for granted, and his recommendations about 'correct pronunciation' (see p. 6) would have been taken on board by every child who had passed through a public school. The absurdity of the opening statement in the article would have been obvious to every reader, even without the respelling of the respected name:

> [T]here is no truth ... in the rules for teaching my fellow-citizens
> to speak English, laid down in the introduction to the pronouncing
> dictionary of Valker.

The writer goes on to defend the idiosyncrasies of Cockney speech, such as the alternation between *w* and *v* heard in the Weller family (p. vii). He claims to use the recent findings of European philology about the way some of the consonant sounds in Indo-European had changed in the first millennium BC to those found in the Germanic languages – as seen in Latin *pater* and English *father*. He then refers to 'Grimm's Canon' (today we call it 'Grimm's Law'), promulgated by the most famous figure of the time, German philologist Jakob Grimm, and asserts that it shows how 'the friendly interchange of the *v*'s and *w*'s, which so pre-eminently distinguishes the Cockney dialect of the English language from all others, is in perfect harmony with the genius of the English language'.

The approach was evidently appreciated, for a second article followed (issue 5, 1843, p. 7), giving a wealth of supportive examples from Germanic, Celtic and Romance. I imagine most of the detail would have gone over the heads of *Punch* readers, but they wouldn't have missed the underlying sarcasm. They would have been hugely amused at the thought that a dialect such as Cockney could ever be taken so seriously.

EMPHATIC!

Boy (*to Nurse*). 'What did you say "made her ill"?'

Nurse. "Ark at you, Halfred! I didn't say, "made 'er HILL"; I said, "she lived at Maida 'ILL"!'

23 March 1861

LEAVING WALKER BEHIND

'Walker' was no descriptive dictionary, recording English in all its diversity. It is strongly prescriptive, with the aim, as Walker says in his preface, for 'the improvement of the English language'. Through his reasoning about the etymology of words, he hoped to stop language change:

> [I]f the analogies of the language were better understood, it is scarcely conceivable that so many words in polite usage would have diversity of pronunciation, which is at once so ridiculous and embarrassing.

The irony, of course, is that several of his recommendations were rejected by polite society. The RP that emerged in the Victorian era differed in several important respects from the norms espoused by Walker.

- One of his four major 'faults' – failing to recognize the distinction between *wh* and *w* – would no longer be maintained (p. 46); today RP speakers make no distinction between *whales* and *Wales*.
- The 'long a' would come to be used in such words as *adv<u>a</u>nce*, *basket*, *chant* and *fast*, making this one of the main markers of the north vs south divide in England. Walker shows them all as having the short vowel a^4, as in *fat*. *Bath*, however, he shows with vowel a^2, as in *far*, anticipating the later fashion.
- The pronunciation of *r* after a vowel would disappear in RP. Walker states very clearly in his introduction that 'This letter is never silent' (p. 56) and he contrasts it with the trilled *r* heard in Ireland. However, he notes a tendency to reduce it to zero: 'it is often too feebly sounded in England, and particularly in London, where it is sometimes entirely sunk'. For him, of course, this was a bad sign.

ONGOING CHANGE

Today RP continues to change, as it has always done, and remains a source of controversy. Most of the issues that caused the Victorians such anxiety have long since been forgotten. Obleege vs oblige? Bal*cony* vs *bal*cony? Chinee vs china? There are hundreds of entries in Walker where the phonetic descriptions differ from those we would find in a present-day pronouncing dictionary. In several instances, he identifies alternative usages that would remain an issue for the Victorians, and be noted in the pages of *Punch*, but most of these had been resolved by the end of the century – to be replaced, of course, by new and equally controversial usages. The first international rodeo pageant took place at Wembley Stadium in London in 1924, which led to furious debate about the word's pronunciation.

PAINFUL SCENE IN A CULTURED SUBURB

The man who pronounced it *Ródeo*.

11 June 1924

80

The rise of the telephone brought with it new forms and new pronunciations, not all of which were appreciated.

New Employee (obtaining telephone number for chief, and using the new pronunciation required by the new official instructions). 'City Fife thr-r-r-ee oh foer. Ha, ha, ha! I say, Sir, don't you feel a most priceless silly ass talking like that?'

14 November 1923

Host (of the newest school). 'What d' yer think o' this nineteen-o-six port?'

Guest (*of the old school*). 'Nineteen-o—! My dear sir, nineteen-*hundred*-and six. We are discussing *wine*, not telephone numbers.'

1922 *Almanac*

But no one could have guessed, in 1922, how pronunciation was about to be affected by the arrival of an even more far-reaching technology than telephones had proved to be. Soon, for the first time in the history of English, the regional accents and varying pronunciations of Britain and beyond would be heard throughout the land.

North-Countryman (to motor-cyclist who has inquired the way). 'Ye coom from Lunnon, don't ye?'

Motor-cyclist. 'Yes.'

North-Countryman. 'A thowt so; ye talk like t' man on t' wireless.'

11 May 1927

FURTHER READING

Cruttenden, A. (ed.), *Gimson's Pronunciation of English*, 7th edn, Hodder Arnold, London, 2008.

Crystal, B., and D. Crystal, *You Say Potato: A Book about Accents*, Macmillan, London, 2014.

Crystal, D., and H. Crystal, *Wordsmiths and Warriors: The English-Language Tourist's Guide to Britain*, Oxford University Press, Oxford, 2013.

Mugglestone, L., *Talking Proper: The Rise of Accent as Social Symbol*, 2nd edn, Oxford University Press, Oxford, 2003.

Wells, J., *Accents of English*, Cambridge University Press, Cambridge, 1982.

PICTURE CREDITS

All photographs are from a private collection, with the exception of the following:

p. 5   John Walker, oil on canvas by Henry Ashby, 1802. © National Portrait Gallery, London.

p. 20   John Walker, watercolour by unknown artist. © National Portrait Gallery, London.

p. 21   Thomas Sheridan by Edmund Scott after Robert Stuart, 1789. © National Portrait Gallery, London.

p. 23   Philip Dormer Stanhope, mezzotint by John Simon after William Hoare, *c*.1742. © National Portrait Gallery, London.

p. 35   From *The Art and Practice of Laundry Work* by Margaret Cuthbert Rankin, *c*.1905, p. 34. © Bodleian Library, University of Oxford.

p. 50   Etching by Thomas Rowlandson, 1768, after Henry William Bunbury; part of *Picturesque Beauties of Boswell*. © Victoria and Albert Museum, London.

p. 81   'New Employee' © Punch.

INDEX